FULL OF SH*T

BAD JOKES AND RANDOM FACTS

WRITTEN BY
LIAM ROBERTSON

Full Of Sh*t: Bad Jokes And Random Facts
Liam Robertson

For permissions contact:
morethanmeetstheeyebook@gmail.com

Book design by Liam Robertson

ISBN 9798869960252 (paperback)

First Edition December 2023

FULL OF SH*T

BAD JOKES AND RANDOM FACTS

WRITTEN BY
LIAM ROBERTSON

FOREWORD

Thanks to modern technology and medical advancements it is now completely normal for people to live well into the age of 80 or 90 years old. This results in a larger population than ever before, with almost 8 billion people on earth today. If the average person lives to the age of 80 - Do you know they will spend as much as 10,000 hours sat on a toilet in their lifetime? That is over 400 days. Over 13 months. Yes, that is a whole year of your life just sat on the toilet. 8 billion people for more than 10,000 hours... that is a lot of toilet time.

Most of us fill this 20 minutes-a-day sit-down quite easily thanks to smart phones and a good wifi connection. The smart phone has become as common a necessity for a visit to the loo as much as the toilet paper we wipe our bums with. I am as guilty as anyone when it comes to smart phone addiction. I would never go to the toilet without my phone. I find it helps me relax and take my time, usually by scrolling through social media or watching the latest viral video.

One day I decided that I should use this 20 minutes each day in a more productive way. So I made it a rule that each day I had to research a topic I didn't know about and educate myself on it. Sometimes history, culture, languages, politics, or sciences like physics and chemistry. I would learn about how black holes are formed or try to memorise the symbols for each chemical element, but mostly it would be random facts that caught my attention.

However, as time went on, I found myself drifting back to videos of people falling over *(which are hilarious)* or social media clips of people telling terrible jokes. It then occurred to me that maybe having a mix of both education and jokes are what is best to stimulate my mind. I decided I would write a book that included both of these things. My hope is that it will maybe distract people from their phones for a while. Educating while also giving something to laugh about to balance it all out.

So, after some deep scientific research *(searching the internet)* I finally put pen to paper *(fingers to keyboard)* and finished the book. So here we are, the best addition to your toilet since double quilted paper.

Full Of Sh*t - Bad Jokes And Random Facts

A BOOK TO BE READ ON THE LOO

In a land where porcelain thrones reign supreme,
Lies a tale of humour fit for your dream.
Welcome, my friend, to this wacky space,
Where time stands still in your secret place.

As you sit upon your throne so grand,
Book in hand, ready to expand
Your knowledge with jokes and curious facts,
Making bathroom breaks the best of acts.

With a chuckle here and a giggle there,
This book will make you quite aware
That the loo isn't just for mundane routines,
But a haven for laughter in between.

Puns that'll make your eyes roll high,
Facts so strange they'll make time fly by.
So delve right in, no need for delay,
Let's make this bathroom the place to stay!

Amidst the silence, the splashes, and sighs,
This book will surely be your prize.
Entertaining, witty, and utterly absurd,
A perfect companion for every word.

So, without further ado, grab a seat,
Let this book make your bathroom complete.
For in these pages, you're sure to find,
Laughs aplenty of the one-of-a-kind kind!

**I was going to start this book with
a joke about chemistry...**

but I was worried it wouldn't get a reaction.

What do you call an overweight psychic?

A four-chin teller.

Nano-Chameleon: Measuring just 28.9 milometers, the smallest known reptile on Earth is the Brookesia nana. Known as 'B', it fits on the tip of a finger and is about the size of a sunflower seed. This tiny new species of chameleon was discovered in a patch of the rainforest in Northern Madagascar.

What do a tick and the Eiffel Tower have in common?

They're both Paris-sites.

M&Ms: This billion dollar business named after Forrest Mars and Bruce Murrie is also known for the controversial relationship between the two businessman. Having both created the candy-coated chocolates, Mars paid Murrie a mere $1 million for his 20 percent share in the company in 1949 – years before M&Ms would become the best selling candy in the US and a billion dollar business.

RANDOM FACTS

My wife is really mad at the fact that I have no sense of direction...

So I packed up my stuff and right.

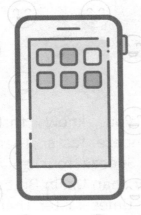

iPhone: I bet you didn't know that the first 'iPhone' was actually made by Cisco and not Apple. Using the voice functions of skype without a computer, the 'Cisco iPhone' was released 22 days earlier than Apple's well known product. Cisco sued Apple for trademark infringement with the lawsuit settled out of court and both companies allowed to keep using the same name. We all know which iPhone became the most popular however.

I regularly dream I am floating in an ocean of orange soda...

It's just a fanta sea.

Sneeze: Did you know that humans can sneeze faster than cheetahs run? Sneeze four an a half times faster than Usain Bolt's record, and 20 times faster than Michael Phelps. Measuring at 100mph, we also expel about 100,000 germs when we sneeze!

I can't believe how expensive it is to go swimming with sharks...

It cost me an arm and a leg.

Close but no cigar: You may have heard the phrase 'close but no cigar' in everyday use when people get close to something but, not quite make it. It stems from the late 19th century where carnival games were targeted at adults instead of kids. Swapping giant teddy bears as the top prize for cigars, if they almost won but didn't earn the prize they'd say 'close but no cigar'.

Have you ever tried to catch some fog?

I tried yesterday but I mist.

RANDOM FACTS

Sea slug: Ever heard of a slug that has the ability to grow a whole new body just from its head? Yup, the sea slug called 'Elysia cf. marginata' is able to survive decapitation and continue to live!

My uncle named his dogs Timex and Rolex...

They're his watch dogs.

Alaskan Wood Frog: Relieving themselves once temperatures increase, Wood Frogs in Alaska can hold their urine for up to 8 months during the region's long winters. This helps them to the survive the freezing winters due to the special microbes in their gut that recycle the urines main waste into nitrogen.

My dog sat on a piece of sandpaper, I asked him how it was...

He said 'Ruff!'

Let your hair down: This famous saying relates back to medieval times where aristocratic women were required to appear in elegant hair-dos that were usually styled up. At the end of the day and in the privacy of their own home, they could finally relax and 'let their hair down' as the saying goes.

After some help I am finally free of my ATM addiction...

I went through a lot of withdrawals first.

Rub the wrong way: Did you know there is a 'right' and a 'wrong' way to clean oak floorboards? During the colonial times, wealthy American homeowners would become annoyed with their servants if they didn't clean their oak floorboards 'the right way'. They believed not wiping the floorboards with dry fabric after wet fabric would ruin their appearance as it caused streaks to form. More modernly used as 'Don't rub the cat the wrong way'.

Did you hear about the emotional wedding?

Even the cake was in tiers.

Tongue Twisters: Dating back as far as the 1800's, The toughest tongue twister in the English language is believed to be The Sheik' Sheep – "sixth sick sheik's sixth sheep's sick" - Can you say that as a quick as you can three times in a row? They most famously appeared in Peter Piper's Practical P Principles of Plain and Perfect Pronunciation. Peter Piper picked a peck of pickled Peppers: Did Peter Piper pick a peck of pickled Peppers?

RANDOM FACTS

I used to hate facial hair...

but then it grew on me.

Dentistry: Did you know that dentistry dates back to 14,000 years ago? The University of Bologna, Italy found a rotten tooth in the jaw of a 14,000-year-old skull had been deliberately sourced and scraped with a tool. Further evidence found teeth being drilled in sulls using a prehistoric bow-drill dating from 7,500 to 9,000 years ago, making dentistry one of the oldest recorded professions known.

I couldn't figure out why the baseball kept getting larger...

Then it hit me.

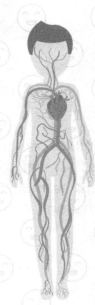

Human circulatory system: If you laid out flat a human's entire circulatory system (veins, arteries, and capillaries) they would stretch for more than 60,000 miles in children, and over 100,000 mile by the time adulthood is reached. This equates to over four times the circumference of the earth.

A cheese factory exploded in France...

Da brie was everywhere.

Go the whole nine yards: When fighter pilots ran out of ammunition in World War II, they knew they had given it their best shot to fight off the enemy as their amo when laid out, measured a total of 9 yards long.

RANDOM FACTS

What's the difference between a hippo and a zippo?

One's pretty heavy and the other's a little lighter.

Wooden wheel: In 2002, in the capital of Slovenia, approximately 12 miles south of Ljublijana, the world's oldest wooden wheel was discovered. It is now displayed in the city's museum, and it is estimated to be somewhere between 5,100 and 5,350 years old as determined by radiocarbon dating.

RANDOM FACTS

How do you organise a party at NASA?

You planet.

Caught red handed: This famous saying originates back to old English law that prevented a person from butchering an animal that wasn't their own. Convictions could only be made however if they were found with animals' blood still on their hands – and therefore catching them in the act of doing something wrong.

What did the pirate say when he turned 80?

Aye matey.

Chef's hat: Did you know that the official name for the tall hats worn by chefs is 'Toque'. A Toque has 100 lines folded into them which are each known as a pleat. He 100 represents the number of ways you can cook an egg.

My wife told me to stop acting like a flamingo...

So I had to put my foot down.

Gruen Transfer: Austrian architect Victor Gruen identified the phenomenon 'Gruen Transfer' which means an intentionally confusing layout in a public venue that could lead to customers spending more time and money in, for example a large shopping centre.

What's the best smelling insect?

A deodor-ant.

Bury the hatchet: This saying dates to the early times in North America where the Puritans conflicted with the Native Americans. To stop conflict and make peace, the Native Americans would bury all their hatchets, knives, clubs, and tomahawks, literally making them inaccessible and a way of ensuring peace.

The problem isn't that obesity runs in your family...

It's that no one runs in your family.

Snoop Dogg: You may or may not know that Snoop Dogg's really name is not Snoop Dogg, but actually Cordozar Calvin Broadus Jr. The nickname he is better known by was given to him by his mother who thought he looked like Snoopy from the Peanuts.

The man who invented knock-knock jokes won an award...

He got a no bell prize.

General Sherman: The largest living thing on earth which is around 2200 to 2700 years old and over 30ft in diameter and almost 300 ft tall in the General Sherman. The Sequoiadendron giganteum is one of three species of coniferous trees known as redwoods and is classified in the family of Cupressacear trees.

I went to buy some camouflage clothes...

But I couldn't find any.

Let the cat out of the bag: In medieval markets, people used to sell piglets in bags for farmers to take home. Sometimes shady dealers would swap the piglet in the back for a less expensive animal like a cat, this exposed the con to everyone but 'letting the cat out of the bag'.

If I got 50p for every failed math exam...

I'd have £6.30 now.

Greenland shark: Older than the Mona Lisa, painted by Leonardo Da Vinci, is the Greenland shark. Researchers who did carbon dating on one they caught in 2014 found it to be around 392 years old. Further testing has revealed that these creatures could be up to 500 years old, meaning they are known as some of the oldest living animals in current day.

250 lbs here on Earth is 94.5 lbs on Mercury...

I'm not fat. I'm just not on the right planet.

Animal fingerprints: Expert crime scene investigators have revealed that Koala prints are very similar to human fingerprints, and they are not alone... Chimpanzees and gorillas also have human like fingerprints. Maybe this helps to explain some of the unsolved crimes in the world.

I hate Russian dolls...

They're so full of themselves.

Cleopatra: The Egyptian queen, lived closer to the release of the iPhone than she did to the building of he pyramids. The pyramids of Giza were built between 2550 BCE and 2490 BCE, by historians' estimates. About 2,421 years later in 69 BCE, Cleopatra, the last active Pharaoh of Ancient Egypt, was born.

When people find out how bad I am as an electrician...

they are shocked.

Bite the bullet: To accept something difficult or unpleasant. In the olden days, when doctors were carrying out treatment on injuries, and were short on anesthesia or in the middle of a battle, they would ask the patient to bite down on a bullet to distract from the pain.

RANDOM FACTS

Geology rocks...

But geography is where it's at.

Butter someone up: To flatter or praise someone as a means of gaining their help or support. This was a customary religious act in ancient India. The devout would throw butter balls at the statues of their gods to seek favour and forgiveness.

Don't you hate it when someone answers their own questions?

I do.

National animal: While Scotland proudly boasts the Loch Ness Monster, one of the world's most famous fabled creatures, the country opted to make another mythical beast its national animal: the unicorn. Although this might seem like an odd choice, Visit Scotland explains that unicorns played an integral role in the country's history. Back in the 12th century, William I used the "proud beast" in the Scottish royal coat of arms.

BAD JOKES

So what if I don't know what "Armageddon" means?

It's not the end of the world.

Most expensive wine: A 73-year-old bottle of French Burgundy became the most expensive bottle of wine ever sold at auction in 2018, going for $558,000 (approx £439,300). The bottle of 1945 Romanee-Conti sold at Sotheby for more than 17 times its original estimate of $32,000.

RANDOM FACTS

I have a few jokes about unemployed people...

but none of them work.

Tittle: That tiny dot above lower case "I" and "j" letters has an actual name: tittle. It is thought that the phrase "to a T" is actually derived from the phrase "to a tittle"—a phrase that was used in the same sense dating back to the early 17th century.

I used to think I was indecisive...

But now I'm not so sure.

Give the cold shoulder: Surprisingly, this doesn't just refer to coldly turning your back on someone. Etymologists think the phrase originated from medieval etiquette. After a feast, hosts in England would subtly signal that the meal was over (and it was time for guests to leave) by serving a cold slice of pork, mutton, or beef shoulder.

RANDOM FACTS

I've just written a song about tortillas...

Actually, it's more of a rap.

Steal someone's thunder: In the early 1700s, English dramatist John Dennis invented a device that imitated the sound of thunder for a play he was working on. The play flopped. Soon after, Dennis noted that another play in the same theater was using his sound-effects device. He angrily exclaimed, "That is my thunder, by God; the villains will play my thunder"

Will glass coffins be a success?

Remains to be seen.

Fire hydrant: The fire hydrant patent is credited to Frederick Graff Sr., who was the chief engineer for Philadelphia Water Works during the early 1800s. Unfortunately for Graff Sr., the patent was destroyed when the patent office in Washington, D.C., burned down in 1836. After 100 years, retired firefighter George Sigelakis reinvented the hydrant after they had been failing to work in too many critical emergencies.

Where do fruits go on vacation?

Pear-is.

Cannibalism: In 16th and 17th century Europe, cannibalism was actually a fairly common practice, and it was all for medical purposes. The practice seems to have started because Egyptian mummies were thought to have magical curative properties—so they were ground up and put in many remedies. As the idea evolved, human bone, blood, and fat were all used in medical concoctions. Got a headache? Crush a skull.

I asked my dog what's two minus two...

He said nothing.

Tornadoes: Tornadoes can develop over water just as well as they can over land. When they do, they're called "waterspouts," and they suck up large amounts of lake or sea water—as well as whatever's swimming in that water. If the waterspout travels on to the land and the winds decrease, there's nowhere for those fish to go but down. As far as we know, there's no tornado powerful enough to pick up sharks, but a fish-nado is entirely possible.

RANDOM FACTS

My wife said I should do lunges to get back in shape...

That would be a big step forward.

Billionaire: The difference between being a millionaire and billionaire is not fully understood by most people. In fact, someone with no money at all is closer to a million, than someone with a million is to a billion. If you are to change the units from from money to time. A million seconds is 11 days, a billion seconds is 31 years. Just let that sink in.

How do you follow Will Smith in the snow?

You follow the fresh prints.

Candy floss: It is not known whether William Morrison had an ulterior motive for inventing the soft confection, but the dentist no doubt helped ensure others in his profession continued drawing in plenty of customers. In 1897, he partnered with candy-maker John C. Wharton to develop the cotton candy machine (which at the time was known as "Fairy Floss"), and it's been bringing kids cavities ever since.

Why don't we see elephants hiding in trees?

Because they're really good at it.

Fly off the handle: In the days before proper manufacturing, poorly fastened axe heads would fall off while they were in use, sometimes mid swing. This would result in the sharp metal object flying through the air. It was dangerous, hence why the phrase is used to describe risky behaviour with unpredictable results.

RANDOM FACTS

What do you call two monkeys that share an Amazon account?

Prime mates.

Giant squid: If you're not fascinated enough by the mystery of giant squids, you should know that they can grow to up to 13 metres long. What's even more scary is that their eyes can be as large as 11 inches across. That makes them the largest known eyes in the animal kingdom.

This graveyard looks overcrowded...

People must be dying to get in.

Human species: Human beings may dominate the planet with our sprawling cities and far-reaching technology, but we are, in fact, just one species among some 8.7 million that live together on planet Earth. One 2011 study published in the journal PLoS Biology estimated that "the various forms of life on the planet included 7.8 million species of animals, 298,000 species of plants, 611,000 species of mushrooms, mould and other fungi, 36,400 species of protozoa, and 27,500 species of algae or chromists." And it's worth noting that the researchers did not venture to put an estimate on the number of bacteria.

I used to be addicted to soap...

But I'm clean now.

Apple pie: Apples originally come from Asia. The first pies were baked in Medieval Europe. Even the concept of putting apples in pie traces back to a recipe from England in 1381. Nevertheless, the phrase "as American as apple pie" turned up by 1924 and became a common saying during the years of the Second World War.

What's the best thing about Switzerland?

I don't know, but the flag is a big plus.

Dogs: Some owners of disobedient dogs may have trouble believing this, but dogs can learn to recognise a vocabulary of about 165 words. Unsurprisingly, dogs respond best to short words, as well as words with hard consonants like "t" or "r," which may explain why they can hear "treat" from three rooms away.

I only know 25 letters of the alphabet...

A B C D E F G
H I J K L M N
O P Q R S T U
V W X Z

I don't know y

Wedding veil: When Maria Paraskeva, a woman from Cyprus, got married in August 2018, her goal wasn't just to say "I do." She was also determined to set a record. "My dream as a child has always been to break the Guinness World Record title for the longest wedding veil," she explained. She fulfilled her dream by wearing a lace veil that stretched 22,843 feet and 2.11 inches, or as long as 63.5 football fields.

What do you call a factory that makes okay products?

A satisfactory.

Oranges: Oranges may be an iconic fruit, but they are not a naturally occurring one, as The Telegraph points out. In fact, oranges are a hybrid of tangerines and pomelos, also known as "Chinese grapefruit," and they were originally green—not, well, orange. Oranges are a subtropical fruit, but now that they exist in more temperate climates, they lose their chlorophyll-induced green and become their more familiar color when the weather warms up.

RANDOM FACTS

What do you call a dinosaur that crashes his car?

Tyrannosaurus Wrecks.

Dandelion: Be careful about drinking any dandelion wine—the French word for dandelion, pissenlit, means "wet the bed." The name comes from the fact that dandelion leaves have diuretic properties.

How does a penguin build its house?

Igloos it together.

Albert Einstein: We all know Albert Einstein as being one of the intellectuals in the history of the human race. Regarded by some as one of the smartest humans to ever have lived. What makes him even more special is his name. An anagram of 'albert einstein' is 'ten elite brains' - coincidence?

What is Forrest Gump's password?

1forest1.

Longest place names: Road signs in Wales tend to be written in both Welsh and English, but some of the more complicated spellings might still flummox you when you're in Wales 'Llanfairpwllgwyngyllgogerychwyrndrobwllllandysiliogogogoch' is one of the longest town names in the world – but don't worry – most people choose to shorten it to the more manageable Llanfairpwll.

My wife asked me to stop singing 'Wonderwall' to her...

I said maybe.

Stone Henge: Stone Henge, located in the south of England, is one of the UK's most famous tourist attractions – Stonehenge was believed to be created in around 3000BC, meaning it's older than Egypt's pyramids.

RANDOM FACTS

How did Darth Vader know what Luke got him for Christmas?

He felt his presents.

Library of Congress: Founded in 1800, the Library of Congress, in Washington DC, is the largest library in the world with more than 173 million items. Closely followed is the national library of the United Kingdom, located in London, which is the second largest library in the world.

What do you call it when James Bond takes a bath?

Bubble 07.

Golf: The sport was invented in St. Andrews, Scotland in the 15th century. In 1457, it was famously banned by King James II because it was interrupting archery practice. Scotland still boasts the finest courses in the world.

Which days are the strongest?

Saturday and Sunday. The rest are weak-days.

Cherophobia: We have all heard of phobias, usually fears of heights or spiders, but have you heard of cherophobia? Do you hate all things fun? People with this phobia tend to avoid any kind of situation that others might classify as fun or joyful.

I hate my job—all I do is crush cans all day...

It's soda pressing.

Saliva: The average person produces roughly one ounce (30 ml) of saliva every hour. That's 24.3 ounces (720 ml) or one full wine bottle's worth of saliva a day, which is an average of 69 gallons (263 liters) per year.

Why is Peter Pan always flying?

Because he Neverlands.

Movie Trailers: The world's first movie trailer was shown at a theater in Harlem, New York, in 1914. The trailer promoted an upcoming movie featuring Charlie Chaplain. The audience would watch the trailer after the movie had ended. The trailers showing after the film was ineffective, as the audience wouldn't stay to watch them.

Did you hear about the restaurant on the moon?

Great food, no atmosphere.

Lion's roar: The lion is commonly known as the king of the jungle, but do you know about its roar? A lion can roar as loud as 114 decibels, roughly 25 times louder than a gas-powered lawnmower. Lions can roar louder than other big cats because of the way their vocal cords are shaped. This allows them to produce more noise with less effort. It can be heard from a far as 5 miles away.

RANDOM FACTS

I was just reminiscing about the beautiful
herb garden I had when I was growing up...

Good thymes.

Turkish coffee: This would be unheard of today, but coffee was an integral part of Turkish society back then. It was introduced into the country in the 15th Century, and by the 16th Century, they had mastered the art of coffee. Coffee became so popular, it seems, that it became grounds for divorce. No one knows why exactly this actually came into law, but the fact remains that it was.

Why did the man fall down the well?

Because he couldn't see that well.

Squirrels: Harmless and cute as they seem, these fuzzy little creatures aren't as innocent as you think. Squirrels tend to chew things, but combine this with power lines, and there's going to be a problem. Squirrel-induced blackouts are much smaller and easier to fix than a blackout caused by a storm, as generally, there's just one cable to repair – there's only so much damage one squirrel can do.

**I only seem to get sick
on weekdays...**

I must have a weekend
immune system.

Sea otter: Sea otters often hold
hands. While it may look like a
couple of otters being adorable,
it's actually a life-saving strategy.
This technique is commonly seen
with mothers and their pups
(that's a baby otter). Another way
they stay still in choppy seas is by
grabbing onto long strands of kelp
that grow up from the seabed.

EPILOGUE

You have now come to the end of "Full Of Sh*t - Bad Jokes And Random Facts - A book to be read on the loo" I hope that you have had some laughs, learned some new things, and maybe even passed the time a little more easily while doing your business. This book was designed to be a fun, lighthearted read that you can pick up and put down at your leisure. I wanted to create a space where you could take a break from the stress of the world and just enjoy some silly jokes and interesting facts.

I hope that you found some of the jokes to be so bad that they were good, and that some of the random facts sparked your curiosity and led you to do some further research on your own.

In the end, I want to thank you for taking the time to read "Full Of Sh*t". I hope that it brought some joy to your day and that you'll pass it on to someone else who may need a laugh or a distraction.

Remember, life is too short to take everything too seriously. So keep reading, keep learning, and keep laughing - even on the loo.

Best regards,

Liam.

REFERENCES

1- **Google** - search engine - (2023)

2- **My imagination** - brain storm - (2023)

COMING SOON

This book is part of a series of more books designed to be read on the loo. Coming soon!